BRITISH
MILITARY
AVIATION
IN THE 1970s

Malcolm Fife

AMBERLEY

First published 2016

Amberley Publishing
The Hill, Stroud
Gloucestershire, GL5 4EP

www.amberley-books.com

Copyright © Malcolm Fife, 2016

ISBN 978 1 4456 5281 8 (print)
ISBN 978 1 4456 5282 5 (ebook)

British Library Cataloguing in Publication Data.
A catalogue record for this book is available from
the British Library.

Typesetting by Amberley Publishing.
Printed in the UK.

Contents

Introduction

The 1970s was a decade of great change for Britain's military air arms. The RAF handed over the role of operating Britain's nuclear deterrent to the Royal Navy in 1969. Its primary role once again became that of providing battlefield and tactical support. For this, new aircraft in the form of Jaguars and Harriers joined the ranks of the RAF. Nimrods replaced Shackletons in guarding Britain's seaways. Several older types were phased out of service including the Belfast, Britannia and Comet. Many other aircraft, however, which were in service in the 1960s lingered on throughout the following decades. The world of the RAF also grew smaller with the withdrawal of the forces east of Suez.

The Royal Navy also had its wings clipped in the 1970s with the retirement of its last large aircraft carrier for fixed-wing aircraft. In its place the vertical take-off and landing Sea Harrier was delivered to the Fleet Air Arm. Helicopters now had a more dominant role. Sea Kings and Wasps operated from nearly all the Royal Navy's warships.

Unlike the other two air arms, the Army Air Corps saw its role expanded in the 1970s and changed from providing purely support to a more offensive nature. Large numbers of new helicopters equipped squadrons in the form of the Lynx and Gazelle, which were capable of being armed. A small number of fixed-wing aircraft were also on strength.

The Americans, who first established air bases in Britain in the Second World War, still retained a large number of combat aircraft in the country. Phantoms and the larger F-111 countered a potential Russian threat when the Cold War was at its height.

This book contains pictures of many of the military aircraft types that could be seen in the skies over the country during that decade.

Royal Air Force

Strike Command

Fighter Squadrons

By the beginning of the 1970s, the threat of a Soviet attack by missiles had superseded that by bombers. At the beginning of the decade the RAF's fighter force was equipped with English Electric Lightnings and American-built Phantoms. The last of the large delta-winged Gloster Javelins had been retired in 1968. The Lightnings based at RAF Leuchars in Scotland were often scrambled to intercept Soviet aircraft flying over the North Sea, close to British airspace.

As the Jaguar became increasingly available for the ground-attack role, the Phantoms which had previously performed it were now deployed for air defence purposes. The Lightnings began to disappear from service from the mid-1970s, with RAF Binbrook hosting the last operational examples of the type.

Overseas, RAF Lightnings provided protection for West German airspace flying from RAF Gutersloh, and there was a single squadron at RAF Akrotiri on Cyprus until 1975.

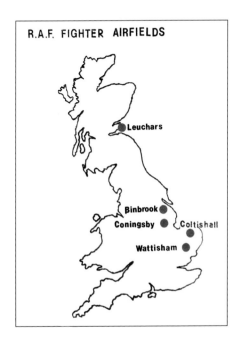

R.A.F. FIGHTER AIRFIELDS

After the Second World War, the RAF's fighter squadrons were concentrated at airfields located on the eastern side of Britain. Throughout the 1950s and 1960s there had been large reductions in the number of fighter aircraft. By the following decade there was only a handful of bases left. In 1974, the last Lightning fighters left RAF Coltishall, with their place being taken by ground-attack Jaguars.

A 111 Squadron Lightning F.3, XR713, at RAF Lakenheath in 1973. The type was the first RAF single-seat fighter to enter service as an integrated weapon system. Airframe systems, engines, armament, fire control radar and auto-controls were all carefully co-ordinated.

Lightning F.6 XS937 of 23 Squadron at RAF Leuchars in September 1971. Just under five years later it crashed into the North Sea off Flamborough, Yorkshire. The pilot ejected when he was unable to lower the undercarriage while on approach to RAF Leconfield.

A formation of four Lightning F.6s of 23 Squadron, XR753, XS937, XR760 and XS935, in 1973.

Four Lightning F6s of 23 Squadron, XR753, XS937, XR760 and XS935, in 1973.

A 5 Squadron Lightning F.3, XR713, in summer 1975. 5 Squadron continued to fly Lightnings until 1987, long after most other squadrons.

A flypast of Lightning F.6s of 23 Squadron and Phantom FG.1s of 43 Squadron at RAF Leuchars on 20 September 1975. Two days earlier, while rehearsing for this, Phantom FG.1 XV580 crashed near Forfar, its two crew ejecting successfully.

In the mid-1970s the RAF's Lightnings lost their characteristic silver appearance. Their bare metal surfaces were painted over in drab colours to camouflage them. One such example is this Lightning F.6, XR772 of 5 Squadron, seen in 1976.

Lightning F.6 XP749 of the Lightning Training Flight, RAF Binbrook, at Prestwick Airport in June 1979.

About to land at RAF Leuchars is a Phantom of 43 Squadron in 1972.

Phantom FG.1 XV571 of 43 Squadron in 1973.

A 43 Squadron Phantom FG.1, XT875, taking off in 1978. The flames in the engines are a result of its afterburners being used to provide additional power.

A Phantom FGR.2, XV501, of 29 Squadron in 1979. It was based at RAF Coningsby for air defence duties.

Phantom XV488 of 228 OCU / Squadron in 1979. It was based at RAF Coningsby in Lincolnshire, where most pilots were trained to fly this type.

In 1919, Alcock and Brown made the first non-stop flight across the Atlantic. To commemorate the sixtieth anniversary of this event in 1979, an RAF Phantom FG2, XV424, re-enacted this flight. For this it was painted in a special colour scheme.

Bomber Squadrons

The most significant change in the RAF's role between the 1960s and the 1970s was the transfer of Britain's nuclear deterrent from land-based bombers to the Royal Navy's submarines. Several squadrons of Vulcans, however, were retained. The Vulcan, with its robust delta wing, was found to be more resilient to flying at low levels than its counterpart the Victor. Although its prime role was to now carry conventional bombs, it could also still be used to deliver nuclear weapons. The RAF had two squadrons of Vulcans based on RAF Akrotiri, Cyprus until they returned to Britain in 1975. In the late 1960s the RAF began to receive Buccaneers to replace the Canberra in the low-level strike role. Like the Vulcans, they were capable of carrying out attacks with either conventional weapons or nuclear bombs. Many of the aircraft were transferred from the Royal Navy but some were new-build machines. Originally it was intended that the British-built TSR2 would replace the Canberra, and even the remaining V-bombers, but this project was cancelled. The American F-111 was ordered instead but this too was cancelled. So the RAF had to make do with the Buccaneer.

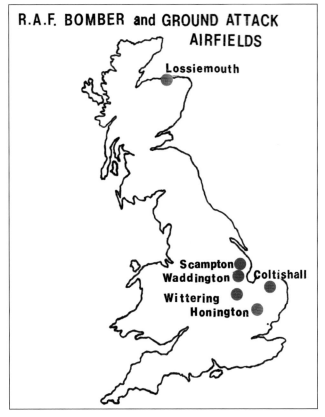

In the 1970s, the RAF's remaining V-bomber squadrons that utilised the Vulcan were concentrated at Scampton and Waddington in Lincolnshire. The Buccaneer squadrons were solely based at RAF Honington. Hunters and later Harriers flew from RAF Wittering. This was the only base in Britain for the revolutionary vertical take-off and landing aircraft. The RAF's other new ground-attack aircraft, the Jaguar, was housed at RAF Coltishall with the training on this type being carried out at RAF Lossiemouth.

Vulcan B.2s had a maximum speed of 645 mph and were usually flown by a crew of five.

Hastings T.5 TG503 of 230 OCU, based at RAF Scampton. Although their task was in the training of bomb aiming, they also undertook patrols over the North Sea.

Vulcan B.2 XL425 of 617 Dambusters Squadron at RAF Lakenheath in June 1973.

237 OCU, which trained Buccaneer S.2 pilots, also had a small number of Hunter T.7s on strength, such as this example pictured in 1974.

The main role of 12 Squadron's Buccaneer S.12As was maritime strike missions. One of its aircraft, XV168, is seen here at RAF Leuchars in 1975.

A 237 OCU Buccaneer S2a, XN977, flying at low level in 1976. A total of 111 Buccaneers served with the RAF.

The folding wings on this Buccaneer S2B, XV354, of 237 OCU at RAF Mildenhall in 1978 give a clue to its origins of this type as a carrier-based aircraft.

Originally the Vulcan was designed to carry out bombing attacks at high altitude. By the 1970s, the increasing effectiveness of surface to air missiles had forced them to fly at low levels to avoid detection. This Vulcan B.2 is pictured in 1978.

Vulcan B.2 XM572 of 35 Squadron at RAF Finningley in 1979.

Vulcan B.2 XM605 of 50 Squadron preparing to take off from RAF Greenham Common in July 1979. In 1981 it was flown to California, where it was preserved.

A Buccaneer S.2, XT284 of 237 OCU, in 1979. The final aircraft for the RAF had been delivered two years earlier.

About to touch down at RAF Greenham Common in 1979 is this Vulcan B.2 of the RAF Waddington wing.

Ground-Attack Squadrons

In the 1960s the Hawker Hunter was the RAF's main ground-attack aircraft. It continued in this role in limited numbers into the early years of the next decade. 8 Squadron was still operating the Hunter FGA.9 and FR.10 in 1971 at RAF Muharraq, Bahrain, in the Middle East. In West Germany, recently delivered Phantom FGR.2s based at RAF Laarbruck had been assigned the task of ground attack in support of the Army. In the 1970s the RAF received a further two new types of ground-attack aircraft, the revolutionary vertical take-off and landing Harrier as well as the Jaguar. Both of these types were deployed in western Germany. In the latter part of the 1970s there were four squadrons of Jaguars here. They took over the ground-attack role from the Phantoms, which were transferred to air defence duties to replace the aging Lightnings. In addition to close air support, both the Harrier and Jaguar could undertake photo reconnaissance of enemy positions. In 1975, six Harrier GR.1s were detached to the British colony of Belize to act as a deterrent to neighbouring Guatemala, which had been displaying hostile intentions towards it.

Jaguar GR.1 XX754, of 226 OCU, in June 1979. 165 single-seat versions of the Jaguar were delivered to the RAF from September 1973 onwards.

The RAF received thirty-eight Jaguar T.2 two-seat advanced operational trainers. This aircraft, XX839, belongs to 226 OCU and is seen landing at Prestwick Airport in 1975.

Harrier GR.3 XV804 of 1 Squadron at RAF Alconbury in June 1975. Two years later this aircraft made an emergency landing at RAF Spitalgate and was damaged beyond repair.

Carrying rocket pods on its wings, this Harrier GR.3, XZ133 of 233 OCU, is seen at RAF Greenham Common having made its first flight only two months earlier.

A Jaguar GR.1, XV762 of 226 OCU, at RAF Leuchars in 1976.

A formation of four Jaguar GR.1s and T.2s of 226 OCU in 1978.

A hovering Harrier GR.3, XV762 of 233 OCU, from RAF Wittering in 1978.

Jaguar GR.1 XX766 of 226 OCU at RAF Mildenhall in 1979.

A Harrier GR.3, XV752, of 233 OCU in 1979.

Maritime Patrol Squadrons

During the Second World War, RAF Coastal Command protected Allied shipping from attacks by German U-boats by operating long-range patrols from British airfields. In the post-war years this role was carried out by the Avro Shackleton, which was a design based on the Lincoln bomber. The type had entered service in 1951 and in 1969 the first of forty-six Hawker Siddeley Nimrods was delivered to replace it. The Shackleton Mk 2 and MR.3, however, continued to patrol the sea lanes until 1972.

The Nimrod then became solely responsible for maritime patrol and rescue until the type was withdrawn in 2010. In the Cod Wars with Iceland in 1972 and 1975/76, RAF Nimrods flew numerous missions in support of the Royal Navy and British trawlers.

The RAF's maritime patrol squadrons were based at just two airfields on mainland Britain. RAF Newquay provided protection to the English Channel and Western Approaches. At the other end of the country was RAF Kinloss, from where most of the Nimrod maritime patrol aircraft operated. Situated in the north of Scotland, it was ideally placed to counter the threat of Soviet naval vessels operating out of Murmansk. The RAF also had one squadron of Nimrods based at RAF Luqa on Malta in the early 1970s.

Throughout the 1970s, Nimrod MR.1s from RAF Kinloss such as this aircraft, XV244, protected the coast around Britain. In the later part of the decade they flew regular patrols over oil rigs and pipeline installations in the North Sea.

A Hawker Siddeley Nimrod MR.1, XV243, at Aberdeen Airport in 1973. The name 'Nimrod' comes from a Biblical character referred to as 'a mighty hunter before the Lord'.

An RAF Kinloss wing Nimrod MR.1, XV247, in 1974. This type had an un-refuelled range of nearly 6,000 miles.

Delivered to RAF Kinloss in 1971, this Nimrod MR.1, XV250, was transferred to Luqa, Malta, the following year. It returned to RAF Kinloss in 1975, where it remained based for the remainder of the decade.

Airborne Early Warning

As with aerial refuelling, airborne early warning was a new post-war task for the RAF. It was first undertaken by the Fleet Air Arm with converted Skyraiders. These were later replaced by the Gannet AEW.3. With the impending withdrawal of the Royal Navy's aircraft carriers, a replacement was sought to provide airborne early warning to counter low-level intruders approaching over the sea. The Avro Shackleton received a new lease of life in this role, the last example having recently been retired from patrolling the sea lanes. Twelve examples were converted to carry airborne early warning radar. All of them were operated by 8 Squadron at RAF Lossiemouth until they were withdrawn from service in June 1991, being replaced by the Boeing AEW.1 Sentry. For most of the 1970s, they operated alongside a small number of Fleet Air Arm Gannet AEW.3s which had been given a reprieve.

On the ground at RAF Waddington in 1978 is Shackleton AEW.2 WL741 *PC Knapweed*.

Shackleton AEW.2 WL790 *Zebedee* of 8 Squadron in 1979. All of the squadron's aircraft were named after characters from the children's television programme *Magic Roundabout*.

An unusual feature of the Shackleton was its contra-rotating propellers. WR963 is seen landing in summer 1979.

Tanker Squadrons

Although experiments in refuelling an aircraft while in flight had been carried out in the 1920s, it was not regularly practiced until after the end of the Second World War. The RAF's first tanker squadron became operational at RAF Marham in 1958, equipped with Vickers Valiants. These had to be hastily withdrawn from service at the end of 1964 when it was discovered their airframes were suffering from metal fatigue. Handley Page Victors were converted from bombers to replace the Valiants. They remained the RAF's main tanker until the early 1980s, when the VC-10 was also used for air-to-air refuelling.

R.A.F. TANKER AIRFIELDS

Marham

From the mid-1960s onwards, RAF Marham in Norfolk was the sole base of the RAF tanker fleet in the form of the Victor K.1 and later the Victor K.2. The airfield continued in this role until the Victor K.2s were retired in 1993.

Built in 1961, this Victor K.2, XL160, was converted from a bomber to a tanker aircraft in the following decade and served with 55 Squadron.

A 57 Squadron Victor K.2, XL231, with Lightning F.6s XR754 and XS901 of 11 Squadron on the end of its fuel hoses.

A Victor K.1 of 214 Squadron at RAF Leuchars in 1971. This unit was disbanded in 1977.

The three hose pipes can be seen trailing from this Victor K.1 in 1972. Smaller aircraft would normally use the wing-tip hoses while larger types would be re-fuelled from the longer hose attached to the fuselage.

A Victor K.1 in 1974. The following year the first K.2s would be delivered to the RAF to replace the K.1.s.

A 57 Squadron Victor K.1, XH651, at RAF Leuchars in 1975.

Above: Victor K.2. XL188 of 55 Squadron at RAF Leuchars in 1976.

Right: The sinister looking nose of Victor K.2 XH669 of 57 Squadron at RAF Finningley in 1979.

Reconnaissance and Electronic Warfare Squadrons

In the early 1970s, spy satellites were still in the early stage of development. Photographic intelligence of enemy territory was still primarily obtained by reconnaissance aircraft. Although the Canberra was being withdrawn from its role as a medium bomber, it would remain in service throughout the 1970s and long after, gathering photographic intelligence. Other types including the Jaguar were also used in this role. 51 Squadron, with its Comets and Canberras, was tasked with gathering electronic intelligence. Radar jamming and training in electronic warfare were undertaken by Canberras of 360 Squadron. This type of aircraft also served in the second-line role of providing targets for RAF combat aircraft to practice their skills on.

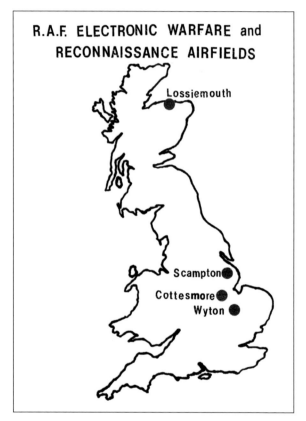

The RAF's only airborne early warning squadron was formed at RAF Lossiemouth in northern Scotland in 1972 and remained at this airfield until it was disbanded in 1991. 98 Squadron flew Canberras from RAF Cottesmore in the electronic calibration role. Argosys and later Andovers of 115 Squadron also performed this role but by the later 1970s had transferred to RAF Brize Norton. Also based at RAF Cottesmore were 360 Squadron's Canberras, which specialised in electronic jamming of radar systems. In 1975, it moved to RAF Wyton, where 51 Squadron was also based. This unit carried out secret electronic intelligence duties with Comets and Canberras. The Comets were later replaced by Nimrods. Photographic reconnaissance was carried out by 39 Squadron Canberras, which were based at RAF Wyton throughout the 1970s. Vulcan SR.2 of 27 Squadron at RAF Scampton carried out strategic maritime radar reconnaissance from 1974. They took over this role from Victor SR.2s of 543 Squadron, which were based at RAF Wyton. A flight of three Victors was retained until May 1975 to monitor French nuclear tests in the Pacific.

Canberra E.15 WH972 of 98 Squadron landing at RAF Leuchars in summer 1972. It was later destroyed in a crash while on approach to RAF Kinloss on 27 June 1990, killing its pilot.

This Canberra B.2, WK119, was operated by 7 Squadron and acted as a target for other aircraft. It is pictured here in 1973, two years before it was retired.

A 360 Squadron Canberra ECM.T.17, WH684, used in the electronic countermeasures role, seen at RAF Leuchars in September 1976.

A 7 Squadron Canberra TT.18, WJ862, at RAF Waddington in June 1978. This version of the Canberra served as a target tug. To ensure it was not mistaken for the target itself, its undersides have been painted black with yellow strips.

A Canberra PR.9, XH167, of 39 Squadron in June 1979, based at RAF Wyton. Although long retired from other front-line roles, the Canberra continued to be used for photo reconnaissance with 39 Squadron until 2006.

Transport and Communications Squadrons

At the outbreak of the Second World War, the RAF only had a handful of transport aircraft. They proved their worth in the conflict, being able to transport troops and supplies long distances at short notice. RAF Transport Command was formed in 1943 and when hostilities ceased it was mainly equipped with C-47 Dakotas. British aircraft manufacturers, however, furnished its requirements in the early post-war years with the Armstrong Whitworth Argosy, Blackburn Beverley and Handley Page Hastings. The American-built Lockheed Hercules, however, began to replace them in late 1968 with only a small number of Argosys surviving into the next decade. The last RAF Argosy was withdrawn from the transport role in 1975 at RAF Akrotiri, Cyprus. With the early retirement of the Andover, the Hercules was the RAF's only tactical transport aircraft in the closing years of the decade.

In 1970 the RAF boasted a substantial fleet of strategic transport aircraft which included Britannias, Comets, Belfasts and VC-10s. With the British withdrawal from East of Suez, there was no longer a need for many of them. Only the VC-10s were retained after 1976. Beagle Bassets, de Havilland Devons, Percival Pembrokes and Hawker Siddeley HS-125s were employed, along with a small number of helicopters in the communications role. Many of the remaining elderly Pembrokes were based at RAF Wildenrath in West Germany.

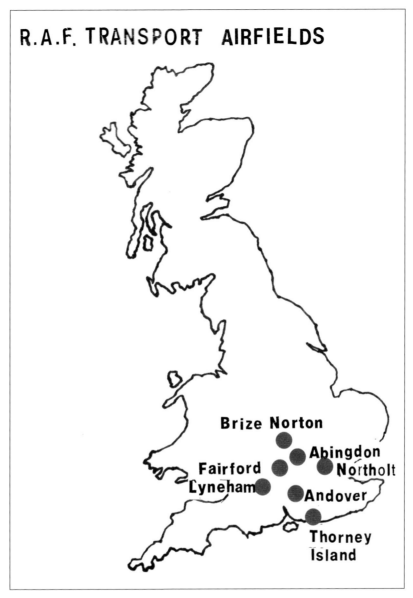

R.A.F. TRANSPORT AIRFIELDS

Brize Norton

Abingdon

Fairford
Northolt

Lyneham

Andover

Thorney
Island

Throughout the 1970s RAF Brize Norton was home to the RAF's strategic transport fleet. VC-10s flew from here throughout this decade. The Britannias and Belfasts which also operated from this airfield, however, had both been withdrawn by the end of 1976. The former type had been based at RAF Lyneham but had moved out in early 1970 to make way for the Hercules. The small number of Comets mainly used for VIP flights, however, remained here until they were withdrawn from service in 1975.

In 1971, the Hercules squadrons based at RAF Fairford departed to join those already at RAF Lyneham. They would remain here for the remainder of the decade and beyond. RAF Andovers C.1 operated from RAF Abingdon in 1970 but later that year they moved to RAF Thorney Island. These twin-engined aircraft remained here until they were withdrawn from service in 1976. The airfield closed soon after. Transport planes continued to use RAF Abingdon throughout the decade for the training of parachutists. The airfield RAF Andover, which had the same name as the transport aircraft, also closed in the mid-1970s. It had been home to 21 Squadron's Devons and Pembrokes. RAF Northolt on the western edge of London then became the sole base for the RAF's communications aircraft, which included Andover CC.2s and H.S. 125s.

The first Short Belfast was delivered to the RAF in 1966. The runways had to be re-enforced at RAF Brize Norton before this large transport aircraft could be based there. Pictured here is XR369, named *Spartacus*.

Most Hawker Siddeley Argosys had been replaced by Hercules in the transport role by 1971. A few were converted to signals duties with 115 Squadron and this example, XR105, seen in 1973, was operated by the Empire Test Pilots' School.

A Beagle Basset CC.1 of 207 Squadron, seen at Edinburgh Airport in June 1971. This type was withdrawn from service there years later. They were less comfortable than the Devons and were plagued by technical problems and lack of spares.

Hercules C.1 XV190 at RAF Lakenheath in 1973. Some sixty-six Hercules C.1s were originally delivered to the RAF but following defence cuts in 1975, thirteen were withdrawn from service.

Short Belfast C.1 XV362, *Sampson*, taking off from Aberdeen (Dyce) Airport in 1973.

The RAF received a total of eight HS-125s in the 1970s for the transport of VIPs and communications purposes. XX506, depicted here in 1974, was operated by 32 Squadron at RAF Northolt, as were all the other aircraft.

Hercules C.1 XV192 from RAF Lyneham becoming airborne in 1974. The Hercules can carry up to ninety-two troops or sixty-four paratroops.

VC-10 XV101 of 10 Squadron in September 1976. All the RAF's VC-10s were named after airman recipients of the Victoria Cross and this aircraft was named *Lanoe Hawker*.

In addition to the Andover C.1, the RAF received a small number of CC.2s for The Queen's Flight and its communications squadrons. XS791 of 32 Squadron is seen here at RAF Leuchars in 1978.

Another view of VC-10 XV101, seen in 1979. This RAF transport could carry 150 troops a distance of 3,670 miles without refuelling.

Coming into land at Prestwick Airport is this Hercules C.1, XV200, in June 1979.

Hercules C.1 XV193 in 1979. Many years later in 1993, it crashed in the Scottish Highlands while carrying out a low flying exercise, killing all nine crew members.

One of the last of the RAF's Hercules to retain its two-tone desert camouflage was XV302, seen here in 1979.

A de Havilland Devon C.2 of 207 Squadron at RAF Finningley in 1979. The last Devon was retired from RAF service in 1984.

Helicopter Squadrons

MAIN R.A.F. HELICOPTER AIRFIELDS

- Aldergrove
- Ternhill
- Shawbury
- Odiham

Left: In Britain, the RAF's Wessex and Puma transport helicopters were concentrated at RAF Odiham, not far from the large army barracks at Aldershot. Some of them were deployed throughout the decade at RAF Aldergrove due to the Troubles in Northern Ireland. Helicopter pilots were trained at RAF Ternhill until 1976, when this role was transferred to RAF Shawbury.

Below: Westland Wessex HC.2 XT672 of 72 Squadron at Prestwick Airport in June 1972.

Westland/Aérospatiale Puma HC.1 XW227 from RAF Odiham in 1973. This type of helicopter had entered RAF service two years earlier.

An air-sea rescue Westland Whirlwind HAR.10 of C Flight, 202 Squadron, at RAF Leuchars in 1974.

Westland/Aérospatiale Puma HC.1 XW208 of 33 Squadron, seen at Duxford Airfield in 1975.

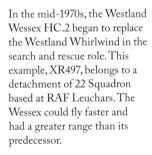

In the mid-1970s, the Westland Wessex HC.2 began to replace the Westland Whirlwind in the search and rescue role. This example, XR497, belongs to a detachment of 22 Squadron based at RAF Leuchars. The Wessex could fly faster and had a greater range than its predecessor.

Based on the American Sikorsky S-58, the Westland Wessex was the RAF's main transport helicopter in the early 1970s. It could carry sixteen soldiers. Pictured at Farnborough in 1978, this Wessex HC.2 was operated by 72 Squadron.

Westland Sea King HAR.3 XZ595 of 202 Squadron at RAF Finningley in 1979. The RAF received its first Sea Kings the previous year to replace the Wessex in the search and rescue role.

Badges

The Tiger's Head was the motif of 74 Squadron. It adorned the tails of its Lightnings up to 1971 when 74 Squadron was disbanded.

A large eagle was displayed on the fin of 23 Squadron's Lightnings in the early in 1970s.

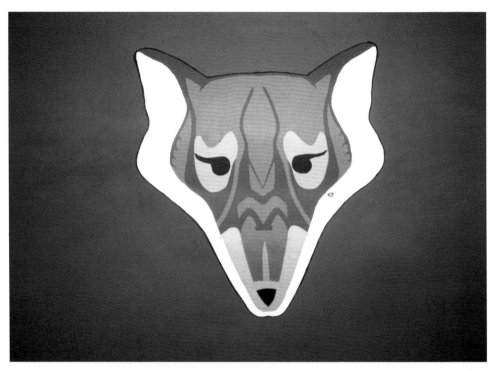

12 Squadron had its emblem, the face of a fox, applied aft of the engine intakes on its Buccaneer S.2s in the 1970s. Before the Second World War, the squadron had been equipped with Fairey Foxes.

This lightning flash on either side of a pair of crossed swords was displayed under the cockpits of 111 Squadron's Phantom FGR.2.

RAF Training Command

In the 1970s, a substantial portion of the RAF's aircraft fleet was devoted to training purposes. The de Havilland Chipmunks which entered service in 1950 were used in the first stage of training pilots. This type was also used by the University Air Squadrons which were located on airfields the length and breadth of Britain. Trainee pilots then graduated to the Jet Provost. Along with the Chipmunk, they were the most numerous type in service in the early 1970s, with around 200 examples of each being flown. The Jet Provost continued in service throughout the decade but the Chipmunk's numbers declined with the delivery of the Scottish Aviation Bulldog. After completing training on the Jet Provosts, new pilots were then streamed onto fast jet training, multi-engine aircraft or helicopters.

Gnats were used in the first role but had been superseded by the Hawk by the end of 1978. Pilots who were to be trained to fly slower multi-engine types first flew the Varsity. It was also used as a flying classroom to train other aircrew including navigators and air electronics operators.

With the reduction in the RAF's bomber and transport aircraft in the mid-1970s, the demand for aircrew fell. The Dominie, which had served alongside the Varsity, now became the RAF's only type to be used as a flying classroom.

The Central Flying School based at RAF Little Rissington was responsible for the training of flying instructors for all three services. In 1976, it was transferred to RAF Valley.

At the beginning of the 1970s, the basic RAF flying training schools equipped with Jet Provosts were located in Yorkshire at RAF Linton-on-Ouse and RAF Leeming. At the end of the decade RAF Church Fenton also received Jet Provosts. In the first few years of the 1970s it had served as the primary flying school, with Chipmunks and later Bulldogs. Other aircrew including navigators were also trained in Yorkshire at RAF Finningley and RAF Topcliffe, although the latter station ceased this function in 1973. RAF Oakington was responsible for training pilots on slower multi-engine aircraft. This role was transferred to RAF Finningley in 1974 and RAF Oakington was handed over to the Army. The RAF College at Cranwell had a fleet of Jet Provosts. On the opposite side of the country, where the air space was less crowded, fast jet training was carried out from RAF Valley. Pilots were then usually sent to RAF Chivenor in Devon, where weapons training was carried out on Hunters. In 1974 this role was transferred to RAF Brawdy but at the end of the decade RAF Chivenor was again used for advanced flying training, this time with Hawks.

R.A.F TRAINING AIRFIELDS

All three services received the
Westland/Aérospatiale Gazelle
in the 1970s, although the RAF
only operated a small number in
the training role.

Delivered in 1966, this Dominie
T.1, XS738, served throughout
the 1970s as a flying classroom.

RAF helicopter pilots were
trained on Westland Whirlwinds
after completing initial
instruction on the Westland
Sioux. This Westland Whirlwind
HAR.10, XN127, pictured
in 1971, was operated by the
Central Flying School, which
was responsible for all RAF
helicopter training.

The Vickers Varsity was
developed to replace the Vickers
Wellington as a flying classroom.
Although the last aircraft had
been delivered to the RAF in
1954, numerous examples were
still in service in the early 1970s.
This Varsity T.1, WF372 of 6
FTS, is seen landing at RAF
Finningley in 1973.

Hawker Hunter F.6 XF383 of 4 FTS, RAF Valley, in 1973. While numerous single-seat Hunters were used for training purposes, most were camouflaged and not painted in Training Command colours like this one.

Although the Hawker Hunter was retired from front-line service in the early 1970s, it continued in service throughout the decade as an advanced jet trainer. This Hunter T.7 was operated by 4 FTS when it was photographed in 1975.

Preparing to take off from Edinburgh Airport in summer 1975 is this Chipmunk T.10, WK585 of 12 Air Experience Flight.

Jet Provost T.4 XS219 of the School of Refresher Flying based at RAF Leeming, pictured in September 1975.

The RAF received its first Scottish Aviation Jetstream in 1973. Some twenty-six were delivered but fourteen were later transferred to the Fleet Air Arm. XX499 is seen taking off in 1976.

The RAF used the Dominie T.1 as a flying classroom. It normally had a crew of six, including a pilot and five pupils and instructors. This example, XS733, one of a small number operated by the RAF College, Cranwell, is seen at RAF Leuchars in 1976.

A Gnat T.1, XR998, from RAF Valley visiting RAF Leuchars in September 1978. This type first entered service in 1962, replacing the Vampire T.11.

Ordered as the RAF's standard trainer to supersede the Chipmunk, the Bulldog first entered service in April 1973. The Yorkshire University Air Squadron had XX619, this example, on strength in 1979.

Jetstream T.1 XX495 of 6 FTS at RAF Finningley in 1979. This type replaced the Varsity for training pilots on multi-engine aircraft.

A 6 FTS Jet Provost T.5B, XW304, in 1979. While most Jet Provosts were used for pilot training, those with 6 FTS at RAF Finningley taught navigators.

Jet Provost T.5 XW309 of 6FTS on approach to RAF Greenham Common in June 1979. The T.5 was the final version of the Jet Provost, with 110 aircraft delivered to the RAF.

British Aerospace Hawk T.1 XX184 of 4 FTS at RAF Finningley in 1979. RAF Valley took delivery of the first Hawk T.1 and by the end of the decade they had replace the Gnat T.1s.

The RAF used numerous examples of the Hawker Hunter throughout the 1970s for training purposes. This aircraft, a Hunter T.7, XL587, is part of the Tactical Weapons Unit formed in 1974 at RAF Brawdy, where pilots were taught low-level flying and combat skills.

RAF Aerobatic Teams

RAF aerobatic teams had their origins in the 1920s. At the prestigious Hendon air displays held on the northern edge of London, formations of aircraft from various squadrons tried to out-perform each other. Machines from the RAF's flying training schools also thrilled the crowds with their aerobatics. Although the Hendon Air Displays came to an end in 1937, aerobatic teams performed at Empire Air Days held at numerous locations throughout Britain until the outbreak of the Second World War. In the 1950s and 1960s, RAF fighter squadrons provided the RAF's premier aerobatic teams. However, with the advent of new aircraft such as the English Electric Lightning, it became increasingly costly as well as impracticable for them to be flown in aerobatic teams.

The Central Flying School had also furnished many outstanding aerobatic teams flying smaller training aircraft. In 1965, they formed the Yellow Jacks, flying Gnat training aircraft. They were soon renamed the Red Arrows and went on to become the RAF's premier aerobatic team, performing at numerous airshows throughout the 1970s. It was not, however, the only RAF aerobatic team in this decade. The Macaws, the Red Pelicans, and the Poachers were among several teams flying Jet Provosts that also thrilled the crowds.

Gnat T.1s of the Red Arrows perform at the Prestwick Air Show in 1975.

Red Arrows Gnat T.1 XP535
about to land in 1979.

A Gnat T.1 of the Red Arrows at
RAF Biggin Hill in May 1979.

The Gnats of the Red Arrows
perform at the Prestwick
Airshow in June 1979.

The Red Arrows Gnats perform
aerobatic manoeuvres over the
East of England Showground
at Peterborough in the summer
of 1979. This was the last year
the team flew the Gnats, with
them being replaced by British
Aerospace Hawks.

The Swords aerobatic team flying Jet Provost T.5s XW370, XW407, XW424, XW426 and XW428 at the Greenham Common Air Tattoo in 1974. This aerobatic team was formed by 3 FTS at RAF Leeming and had only a brief existence of one season.

A line astern formation of the Poachers aerobatic team from RAF Cranwell, seen here in 1972 flying Jet Provosts XW373, XW353, XW363 and XW359. The team was disbanded in 1976 due to economic reasons. The Poachers was the RAF's last Jet Provost aerobatic team.

Jet Provost T.5 XW375 of the Poachers aerobatic team in 1976.

The Gemini Twins aerobatic team in 1973, flying Jet Provost T.5s XW407 and XW410. Their home base was RAF Leeming.

By the early 1970s, all Vampires and almost all Meteors had been phased out of service with the RAF. The Central Flying School, however, maintained one example of each type in flying condition which continued to appear at air shows under the name 'The Vintage Pair': Meteor T.7 WA669 and Vampire T.11 XH304.

Meteor T.7 WA669 of the CFS Vintage Pair at RAF Lakenheath in 1973.

Fleet Air Arm

In 1964, no fewer than 140 F-4 Phantoms were ordered for the Fleet Air Arm. It was intended to operate them from HMS *Ark Royal* and HMS *Eagle,* as well as a newly built super-carrier in the next decade. Two years later, defence cuts planned to end all fixed-wing flying by the beginning of the 1970s. With a change of government, one aircraft carrier, HMS *Ark Royal*, was given a reprieve. It remained in service until 1978, when the Royal Navy began to receive new carriers from which the vertical take-off and landing Sea Harriers were to operate.

With the reduction of fixed-wing flying, the Fleet Air Arm also lost many of its second-line squadrons which had been used to train pilots in this role. Helicopter squadrons now dominated its ranks. Almost every ship in the Royal Navy was now capable of operating at least one Sea King, Wessex or Wasp. These were usually used in the submarine hunting role. The Fleet Air Arm also had a sizeable force of Wessex helicopters to provide transport for the Royal Marines in amphibious assault operations. Two former aircraft carriers, HMS *Hermes* and HMS *Bulwark*, had been converted for this role and were each capable of embarking a squadron of Wessexes.

The Fleet Air Arm had a small number of airfields to house its aircraft and helicopters when their ships were not at sea. It started the 1970s with three airfields for its carrier-based aircraft: RNAS Brawdy, RNAS Lossiemouth and RNAS Yeovilton. By the end of the decade the first two airfields had been transferred to the RAF. Only Yeovilton remained as a base for the Sea Harriers. Helicopter pilots were trained at RNAS Culdrose and RNAS Portland, which had no runways, was where many ship-based helicopters disembarked. The Royal Navy's Sea Heron and Sea Devon communications aircraft flew out of RNAS Lee-on-Solent.

Fixed-Wing Squadrons

Two aircraft of the Phantom Training Unit based at RAF Leuchars to train pilots for 892 Squadron in the early 1970s.

Throughout most of the 1970s, 849 Squadron operated a small number of the early versions of the Gannet, including this T.5 seen in the summer 1973, alongside their Gannet AEW.3s.

A Buccaneer of 809 Squadron in 1973.

Two Phantom FG.1s of 892 Squadron, XT863 and XT868, in 1975. This was the Fleet Air Arm's only operational Phantom squadron. It flew from the carrier HMS *Ark Royal* until it was withdrawn from service in 1978.

Fairey Gannet AEW.3 XL471 of 849 Squadron at Prestwick Airport in June 1975. The large pod under the fuselage houses the radar.

In 1975, the Blue Herons aerobatic team were formed by the FRADU at Yeovilton, flying Hunter G.A.11s. They are seen here in 1976 flying WT806, WT804, WW654 and WV267.

The last Sea Vixen FAW.2s in front-line service were those in 899 Squadron which operated from the carrier HMS *Eagle*, which was withdrawn from service in 1972. A number remained in service with the RAE Bedford, including this example, XN653, seen at RAF Greenham Common in 1976.

809 Squadron Buccaneer S.2s XT273, XV337 and XV344 in 1973. Most of the Royal Navy's Buccaneers were transferred to the RAF but the Fleet Air Arm retained around twenty aircraft until end of 1978.

De Havilland Sea Heron C.4 XM296 landing at Biggin Hill airfield in 1979. This aircraft was assigned to the Flag Officer, Naval Air Command and was known as the 'Admiral's Barge'.

In the 1960s, the Fleet Air Arm had a fleet of Hunter GA.11s to train pilots. With the demise of most fixed-wing flying in the following decade, they were no longer needed. Some Hunter GA.11s were retained by the FRADU to provide targets for warships, including this aircraft, XT804, seen here in 1979.

The tail of an 849 Squadron Fairey Gannet AEW.3 adorned with the unit's markings, which include a large wasp.

One of the most significant developments in British military aviation at the end of the 1970s was the introduction of the Sea Harrier and new aircraft carriers from which they could operate. This Sea Harrier, XV457, was delivered in December 1979.

The Fleet Air Arm received fourteen Jetstream T.2s to train observers for their helicopters. XX489 is seen here at Prestwick Airport in 1979.

Phantom FG.1 XV592 of 892 Squadron at RAF Leuchars, which was its home base when not embarked on HMS *Ark Royal*.

Helicopter Squadrons

In 1969 the Fleet Air Arm received its first Sea Kings to replace the Westland Wessex. XV707, a Sea King HAS.1, is seen here in 1976.

Westland Wasp XT784 at Rosyth Naval Base in 1978. It was attached to the Leander Class frigate HMS *Cleopatra*.

The Fleet Air Arm received a small number of Gazelles for training purposes. This one, XX397, was used by the Sharks helicopter display team in 1979.

Westland Sea King HAS.2s XV661 and XV674 of 819 Squadron in 1979. This unit was stationed at Prestwick Airport to guard the approaches to the Firth of Clyde which were used by the nuclear submarine fleet at Faslane.

Army Air Corps

Since the earliest days of warfare, being forewarned of your enemy's positions and movements would give you a tactical advantage. In the Boer War the British Army used gas balloons with observers to spy on its adversaries. This progressed to manned aircraft operated by the Royal Flying Corps in the First World War. With the formation of the RAF the gathering of information from the air on the activities of hostile armies now became the responsibility of this service. During the Second World War, Westland Lysanders and later Austers were employed in what became known officially as Air Observation. A new innovation in the form of the helicopter began to enter service at the end of the war. In time it began to replace fixed-wing aircraft in the observation role. The Army Air Corps was formed in 1957 and assumed the role of directing artillery fire and some forms of aerial reconnaissance. A small number of fixed-wing aircraft were also operated for light transport duties. Throughout the 1970s, the Army Air Corps received large numbers of new helicopters in the form of the Gazelle and Lynx. Both types of machines could carry weapons, unlike the machines they replaced. The Lynx could also carry small number of soldiers.

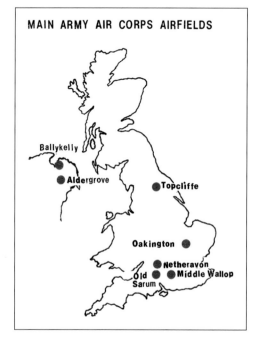

MAIN ARMY AIR CORPS AIRFIELDS

Ballykelly
Aldergrove
Topcliffe
Oakington
Netheravon
Old Sarum
Middle Wallop

The Army Air Corps' main airfield was at Middle Wallop. Unlike most other military airfields at that time, it still possessed grass runways. Pilots were trained here on both fixed-wing aircraft and helicopters. Every type flown by the Army Air Corps could be found here, e.g. Chipmunks, Beavers, Sioux, Scouts, Gazelles. A further two small airfields in the region were also operated by the Army Air Corps, namely Netheravon and Old Sarum. The latter, however, ceased to be used in 1979. The Army Air Corps also had a significant presence at RAF Aldergrove in Northern Ireland to counter the activities of terrorists which continued for the duration of the 1970s. There were also small numbers of helicopters at other locations including RAF Topcliffe and in the late 1970s at Oakington.

The Army Air Corps had a major presence in West Germany to support the British troops deployed there. There were also small numbers of helicopters scattered across the globe from Canada in the west to Hong Kong in the east.

The Army Air Corps received forty-six de Havilland Beavers in the early 1960s. This Canadian aircraft was designed for operating from short airstrips. In the 1970s it was used extensively in Northern Ireland in the photo reconnaissance role. This example, XV268, is seen in Middle Wallop in 1971.

The Chipmunk T.10 was used by the Army Air Corps as a basic trainer aircraft for all pilots, including those who would go on to fly helicopters. WD325 is seen here in 1971 at Middle Wallop, where it was based.

Basic helicopter training for the Army Air Corps was carried out by a civil contractor, Bristow Helicopters, which had a fleet of Bell-47s based at Middle Wallop including this machine, G-AXKZ, pictured in 1975.

A formation display by Chipmunk T.10s of the Army Air Corps at Middle Wallop in July 1975.

Throughout the 1970s, the Westland Scout AH.1 was widely deployed by the Army Air Corps. It could be armed with two machine guns fitted to its undercarriage skids. This example, XR600, was based at Middle Wallop, where it is seen flying in 1975.

A Westland Scout AH.1 of the Army Air Corps becoming airborne in September 1976.

By the late 1970s, the Army Air Corps had replaced its Sioux helicopters with the Westland/Aérospatiale Gazelle. This machine, WX847, was based at Middle Wallop when this picture was taken in 1979.

In the closing years of the decade, the AAC only had around a dozen or so Beavers in service. XP820, pictured here, is seen landing at Biggin Hill airfield in 1979 and by this time had been relegated to the Museum of Army Flying.

Army Air Corps Westland Lynx AH.7 XZ178 in 1979. The orange patch on it indicates it is used in the training role.

Test and Research Establishments

In the 1970s, the British government funded a not inconsiderable fleet of aircraft to carry out research and development in many fields of aviation. They were usually former RAF or Fleet Air Arm aircraft and continued to display military markings. Sometimes types that had been retired from military service continued to fly on with the research establishments for many years. The Royal Aircraft Establishment was the main organisation which carried research into aerodynamics, structures, aviation electronics and weapons. Occasionally it received aircraft such as the BAC-111 airliner, which did not have an earlier military career. It also had a small fleet of de Havilland Doves to transport staff and equipment to the more remote RAE airfields. The Aeroplane & Armament Establishment at Boscombe Down was responsible for acceptance testing of all military aircraft and associated equipment intended for use by the British Armed Forces. It was also home to the Empire Test Pilots' School which trained pilots in this skill from around the world.

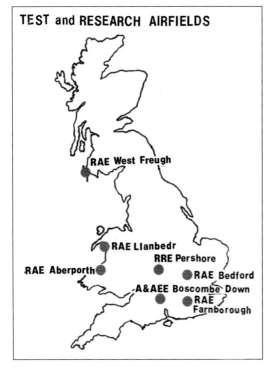

TEST and RESEARCH AIRFIELDS

RAE West Freugh

RAE Llanbedr

RRE Pershore

RAE Aberporth

RAE Bedford

A&AEE Boscombe Down

RAE Farnborough

By far the best known airfield assigned for test and research purposes was RAE Farnborough. The RAE also had a substantial fleet of aircraft at RAE Bedford. Of the other airfields, RAE Aberporth and RAE Llanbedr in Wales were used for missile tests and RAE West Freugh in Scotland for weapons testing on nearby ranges. A&AEE Boscombe Down was mainly concerned with evaluating and testing military aircraft. Unlike the previous establishments, the Royal Radar Establishment at Pershore did not see out the decade, closing in 1977 with most of its aircraft moving to RAE Bedford.

The nose of the Meteorological Research Flight's Hercules W.2, XV208, which was transferred from the RAF in 1972 and modified by Marshalls of Cambridge. It was nicknamed 'Snoopy' and was based at RAE Farnborough.

The Scottish Aviation Twin Pioneer was a short take-off and landing transport aircraft which was mainly used in the Middle East. By the end of the 1960s it had been withdrawn from service but the Empire Test Pilots' School continued to use XT610, shown here, until 1975.

RAE Hawker Hunter T.7 XL612, pictured in 1976. A number of Hunters were operated by this organisation, with this aircraft based at RAE Bedford.

The Royal Radar Establishment at Pershore used this hybrid Meteor NF.11, WD790, for a variety of trials and it was fitted with a TSR.2's nose cone including the radar intended for that type. It is seen here at Greenham Common in 1976.

Transferred from BOAC in 1967, this de Havilland Comet, XV814, served with RAE until it was retired in 1993. In March 1977, it was painted in the raspberry ripple colour scheme adopted by most RAE aircraft around about that time. The RAE had several other examples on strength in the 1970s and the RAF operated five examples in the transport role in the early part of the decade.

The RAE at Farnborough had several Westland Wessexes including XM330, pictured here in 1978.

Although the C-47 Dakota was retired from RAF service in 1970, the RAE continued to operate this example, KG661, throughout the next decade at RAE West Freugh in Scotland. It is depicted here at RAF Mildenhall in June 1979. The following month it unusually received a new serial number, ZA947, as it was discovered that the aircraft had been wrongly identified when purchased for the RAE. The original Dakota KG661 had crashed in Canada in 1944.

A Beagle Basset CC.1, XS770, of the Empire Test Pilots' School at RAF Finningley in 1979. It only retired in 2014, after forty-six years' service.

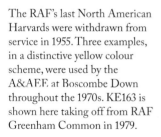

The RAF's last North American Harvards were withdrawn from service in 1955. Three examples, in a distinctive yellow colour scheme, were used by the A&A.E.E. at Boscombe Down throughout the 1970s. KE163 is shown here taking off from RAF Greenham Common in 1979.

Although the Varsity was drawn from RAF service in 1976, a small number were still flying with research establishments at the end of the decade. WF379 with its elongated nose was one of them.

US Air Force

During the Second World War, a large number of airfields were constructed in Britain from which the US Eighth Air Force launched bombing raids on Germany. When hostilities ended, the Americans remained.

Britain was regarded as a useful asset, an unsinkable aircraft carrier, to help contain the Communist USSR. Strategic Air Command eventually withdrew its deployments of nuclear armed B-47s in 1966, but an increasing obsolete force of tactical aircraft remained. Phantoms began to arrive during the previous year and by the early 1970s were the main type based in Britain. They were joined by the F-111s of the 20th Tactical Fighter Wing, the name being somewhat misleading as they were capable of carrying out bombing missions with nuclear weapons. Britain's importance as a base for US Air Force squadrons gained added significance with France's withdrawal from NATO in 1966. Some of the units were redeployed to Britain. Despite often housing exclusively American squadrons, the airfields were still nominally under the control of the Ministry of Defence as they were each commanded by an RAF officer and were referred to as RAF airfields, for example RAF Mildenhall.

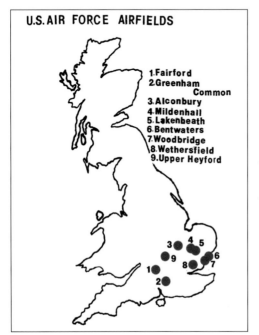

U.S. AIR FORCE AIRFIELDS

1. Fairford
2. Greenham Common
3. Alconbury
4. Mildenhall
5. Lakenheath
6. Bentwaters
7. Woodbridge
8. Wethersfield
9. Upper Heyford

In the Second World War, the airfields of the US Army Air Force were concentrated in East Anglia. Most of the US squadrons deployed in Britain in the 1970s were still located in this region. RAF Wethersfield lost its aircraft to Upper Heyford at the beginning of the decade. No aircraft were based at RAF Greenham Common and it was primarily a reserve airfield. In the early 1970s, Concorde flew test flights from RAF Fairford but these had ceased by the time USAF aircraft arrived here in 1977. RAF Mildenhall housed the transport and tanker aircraft. It also served as a staging post for US aircraft heading for Continental Europe or further east.

1976 was the 200th anniversary of the American Declaration of Independence and to commemorate this event General Dynamics F-111E 68-0028 of the 20th TFW, RAF Upper Heyford, was painted in a special colour scheme.

A formation of Phantoms of the 81st TFW based at RAF Bentwaters and RAF Woodbridge.

Throughout most of the 1970s, F-111s and Phantoms were the main USAF types based in Britain. In 1978, the A-10, designed for close air support missions, began arriving at RAF Bentwaters and RAF Woodbridge. These two are 77-0231 and 77-0234 of the 81st TFW.

A General Dynamics F-111E, 68-0054 of the 20th Tactical Fighter Wing based at RAF Upper Heyford, pictured in 1979. 50 F-111s were ordered for the RAF but due to a retrenchment of government expenditure, the order was cancelled in 1968.

A USAF HC-130 Hercules of the 67th Air Rescue and Recovery Squadron landing at RAF Greenham Common in July 1979. This was the only USAF unit to have Hercules aircraft based in Britain. Operating out of RAF Woodbridge, 67 ARRS were capable of carrying out rescue missions far out to sea as well as special operations.

A display of variable geometry by F-111s of the 20th TFW from RAF Upper Heyford in 1979.

Some of the USAF Phantoms based in Britain were used in the photo-reconnaissance role, such as this RF-4C, 68-0568, from RAF Alconbury photographed in June 1979.

Appendix

Air Stations and Aircraft
as at Autumn 1973

The following list was compiled from contemporary sources. It is intended to provide a comprehensive overview of all aspects of British military aviation at this point in time. Some of the numbers given for aircraft types on strength are approximate. Where no figure is indicated, the total is not known.

Royal Air Force

Aircraft in Service

1 Auster AOP.6
13 Avro Shackletons (MR.2s and AEW.2s)
60 Avro Vulcan B.2s
1 Beagle Husky
16 Beagle Basset CC.1s
9 Bell Sioux HT.2s
20 Bristol Britannias (C.1s and C.2s)
180 de Havilland Chipmunk T.10s
8 de Havilland Comets (C.2s and C.4s)
22 de Havilland Devons
125 English Electric Canberras (B.2s, T.4s, B(I).8s, PR.9s, E.15s, T.17s, TT.18s, T.19s)
140 English Electric Lightnings (F.1s, F.2s, F.3s, T.4s, F.5s, F.6s)
4 Gloster Meteors
8 Handley Page Hastings T.5s
40 Handley Page Victors (B.2s, BSR.2s and K.1s)
100 Hawker Hunters (F.6s, T.7s and FGA.9s)
25 Hawker Siddeley Andovers (C.1s and CC.2s)
11 Hawker Siddeley Argosys (C.1s and E.1s)
40 Hawker Siddeley Buccaneer S.2s
19 Hawker Siddeley Dominie T.1s
4 Hawker Siddeley HS.125 CC.1s
70 Hawker Siddeley Gnat T.1s
70 Hawker Siddeley Harriers (GR.1s and T.2s)
41 Hawker Siddeley Nimrod MR.1s
200 Hunting Percival Jet Provosts (T.3s, T.4s and T.5s)
14 Hunting Percival Pembrokes

130 McDonnell Douglas Phantoms (FG.1s and FG.2s)
59 Lockheed Hercules C.1s
6 Sepecat Jaguar GR.1s
30 Scottish Aviation Bulldog T.1s
3 Scottish Aviation Jetstream T.1s
10 Short Belfast C.1s
50 Vickers Varsity T.1s
36 Westland/Aérospatiale Puma HC.1s
45 Westland Wessexes (HC.2s and HCC.4s)
4 Westland Gazelle HT.3s
60 Westland Whirlwind HAR.10s

RAF Training Command

HQ RAF Brampton, Cambridgeshire.

Varsity WF372, 6 Flying Training School, at RAF Finningley in 1973.

Air Cadets were given flying experience in Chipmunk T.10s such as WB567 of 12 AEF at RAF Leuchars in 1972.

A Gnat T.1, of 4 Flying Training School, RAF Valley. The first course on this type commenced here in early 1963 and it continued in use until 1978 when it was replaced by the Hawk. This example, XM706, is seen at RAF Leuchars in 1976.

Jet Provost T.5 XV302 of 1 FTS, RAF Linton-on-Ouse, in 1972.

A formation of types used by the RAF Training Command including two Varsities, two Dominies and a Jet Provost at RAF Finningley in 1973.

Flying Training Schools
RAF Linton-on-Ouse, Yorkshire
(Relief landing ground: RAF Elvington)
No. 1 FTS (Basic Flying Training) (38 Jet Provost T.3s and T.4s)

RAF Church Fenton, Yorkshire
(Relief landing ground: RAF Rufforth)
No. 2 FTS (Primary Flying Training) (26 Chipmunk T.10s, 10 Bulldog T.1s)

RAF Leeming, Yorkshire
(Relief landing ground: RAF Disforth)
No. 3 FTS (Basic Flying Training) (30 Jet Provost T.3s and T.5s)

RAF Valley, Anglesey
(Relief landing ground: RAF Mona)
No. 4 FTS (Advanced Flying Training) (40 Gnat T.1s and 15 Hunter F.6s and T.7s)

RAF Oakington, Cambridgeshire
(Relief landing ground: RAF Waterbeach)
No. 5 FTS (Multi-Engined Aircraft Flying Training) (28 Varsity T.1s)

RAF Finningley, Yorkshire
No. 6 FTS (Navigational Training) (13 Dominie T.1s, 10 Varsity T.1s, 8 Jet Provost T.4s)

Other Training Command Airfields
RAF Cranwell, Lincolnshire
(Relief landing ground: RAF Barkston Heath)
Royal Air Force College (50 Jet Provost T.3s and T.5s, 2 Chipmunk T.10s)

RAF Manby, Lincolnshire
College of Air Warfare (6 Dominie T.1s, 18 Jet Provost T.4s)
(Aircraft left in December 1973)

RAF Topcliffe, Yorkshire
Air Electronics and Flight Engineers' School (12 Varsity T.1s)
(Air Electronics and Flight Engineers' School transferred to RAF Finningley at end of 1973)

RAF Little Rissington, Gloucestershire
(Relief landing ground: RAF Aston Down)
Central Flying School (training of instructors) (17 Jet Provost T.3s, 6 Chipmunk T.10s, 5 Bulldog T.1s, 2 Varsity T.1s)

RAF Kemble, Gloucestershire
Central Flying School and base of Red Arrows aerobatic team (20 Gnat T.1s)

RAF Ternhill, Shropshire
(Relief landing ground: RAF Chetwynd)
Central Flying School (helicopter training) (9 Sioux, 16 Whirlwind HAR.10s, 4 Gazelle HT.3s)

RAF Shawbury, Shropshire
Air Traffic Control School (14 Jet Provost T.4s)

RAF Training Command Aerobatic Teams

Red Arrows	9 Gnat T.1s	CFS Kemble
Red Pelicans	4 Jet Provost T.4s	CFS Little Rissington
The Linton Blades	4 Jet Provost T.5s	1 FTS, Linton-on-Ouse
The Blue Chips	2 Chipmunk T.10s	2 FTS, Church Fenton
The Gemini Twins	2 Jet Provost T.5s	3 FTS Leeming
The Dragons	3 Hunter F.6s	4 FTS, Valley
	1 Hunter T.7	
The Poachers	4 Jet Provost T.5s	RAF College, Cranwell
The Macaws	4 Jet Provost T.4s	College of Air Warfare, Manby
The Vintage Pair	1 Meteor T.7	CFS Little Rissington
	1 Vampire T.11	

University Air Squadrons and Cadet Air Experience Flights

Abbotsinch Airport, Renfrewshire
Glasgow and Strathclyde UAS (5 Chipmunk T.10s)

RAF Abingdon, Oxfordshire
6 AEF and London UAS (16 Chipmunk T.10s)

RAF Bicester, Oxfordshire
Oxford UAS (6 Chipmunk T.10s)

RAF Church Fenton, Yorkshire
9 AEF and Yorkshire UAS (12 Chipmunk T.10s)

Dyce Airport, Aberdeen
Aberdeen UAS (4 Chipmunk T.10s)

Exeter Airport, Devon
4 AEF (2 Chipmunk T.10s)

Filton Airfield, South Gloucestershire
3 AEF and Bristol UAS (10 Chipmunk T.10s)

Hamble Airfield, Hampshire
Southampton UAS (6 Chipmunk T.10s)

RAF Newton, Nottinghamshire
7 AEF and East Midland UAS (9 Chipmunk T.10s)

RAF Manston, Kent
1 AEF (5 Chipmunk T.10s)

RAF Ouston, Northumberland
11 AEF and Northumbrian UAS (6 Chipmunk T.10s)

RAF St Athan, Vale of Glamorgan
University of Wales UAS (4 Chipmunk T.10s)

RAF St Mawgan, Cornwall
2 AEF (4 Chipmunk T.10s)

RAF Turnhouse, Edinburgh
12 AEF and East Lowlands UAS (10 Chipmunk T.10s)

RAF Shawbury, Shropshire
8 AEF and Birmingham UAS (8 Chipmunk T.10s)

RAF Aldergrove, Northern Ireland
13 AEF (- Chipmunk T.10s)

Teversham Airfield, Cambridgeshire.
5 AEF and Cambridge UAS (9 Chipmunk T.10s, 1 Husky)

RAF West Malling, Kent
London UAS (- Chipmunk T.10s)

RAF White Waltham
(London UAS Chipmunks transferred to RAF Abingdon)

RAF Woodvale, Merseyside
10 AEF and Liverpool and Manchester UAS (10 Chipmunk T.10s)

RAF Strike Command

HQ RAF High Wycombe

No. 11 Fighter Group
HQ RAF Bentley Priory, London

The de Havilland Dove was adopted for RAF service in 1948 and was named in its military guise the Devon. Its primary role was that of a staff transport. This aircraft is a Devon C.2 of 207 Squadron at RAF Greenham Common in 1974.

A Hawker Siddley Andover C.1, XS612, of 46 Squadron in 1974. It could carry forty-four troops or twenty-six paratroops.

In the 1970s, the RAF's VC-10s were purely used in the transport role. Unlike civil airliners, the passenger seats all faced backwards to enhance safety. This example, XV141 of 10 Squadron, is seen in the summer of 1973.

Hercules C.1 XV181 with its loading ramp down at the rear end of the fuselage. Paratroops or military equipment could be dropped from it.

Lightning F.1 XM180 of 226 OCU / 65 Squadron from RAF Coltishall, seen at Prestwick Airport in June 1972. It ended its life as a decoy aircraft at RAF Gutersloh, West Germany, in the late 1970s.

Originally used as a long-range transport aircraft in the 1950s and 1960s, the Handley Page Hastings was still in service in 1972 when this picture of TG568 was taken. By then the handful still in service were used by Strike Command to train bomb aimers.

Nimrod MR.1 XV248. This type's design was based on the de Havilland Comet airliner.

A 57 Squadron Victor K.2 tanker, XA669, at RAF Finningley in September 1979. The Victor was longest serving RAF V bomber, with the first example delivered in 1957 and the last example being withdrawn in 1993 when the VC-10 replaced it in the tanker role.

Photographed shortly before its retirement from the strategic reconnaissance role in 1974 is this Victor SR.2 of 543 Squadron.

A Puma HC.1 and Wessex HC.2 transporting artillery pieces in 1973.

A Vulcan B.2, XH557, of 50 Squadron seen in 1973.

RAF Leuchars, Fife
23 Squadron (15 Lightnings)
43 Squadron (12 Phantom FG.2s)
OCU (5 Phantom FG.2s)

RAF Binbrook, Lincolnshire
5 Squadron (14 Lightning F.6s)
11 Squadron (14 Lightning F.3s and F.6s)
Target Flight Facility (3 Lightnings)

RAF Wattisham, Suffolk
29 Squadron (14 Lightning F.3s)
111 Squadron (14 Lightning F.3s and F.6s)
Target Flight Facility (3 Lightning F.1s)

No. 18 Maritime Group
HQ RAF Northwood, Hertfordshire

RAF Pitreavie Castle, Fife

RAF Kinross, Moray
120 Squadron (5 Nimrod MR.1s)
201 Squadron (5 Nimrod MR.1s)
206 Squadron (5 Nimrod MR.1s)

RAF Lossiemouth, Moray
8 Squadron (12 Shackleton AEW.12s)

RAF St Mawgan, Cornwall
42 Squadron (6 Nimrod MR.1s)

Search and Rescue Flights
(Usually each equipped with 2 Whirlwind HAR.10s)
22 Squadron: Flights at RAF Chivenor, RAF St Mawgan, RAF Valley
202 Squadron: Flights at RAF Acklington, RAF Coltishall, RAF Leconfield, RAF
Leuchars, RAF Lossiemouth

No. 1 Bomber Group
HQ RAF Bawtry, Yorkshire

RAF Scampton, Lincolnshire
617 Squadron (8 Vulcan B.2s)
27 Squadron (Reforming with Vulcan B.2 MRRs)

RAF Waddington, Lincolnshire
44 Squadron (8 Vulcan B.2s)
50 Squadron (8 Vulcan B.2s)
101 Squadron (8 Vulcan B.2s)

RAF Honington, Suffolk
12 Squadron (12 Buccaneer S.2s)

No.90 Signals Group
RAF Cottesmore, Rutland
98 Squadron (7 Canberra E.15s)
115 Squadron (8 Argosy E.1s)
360 Squadron (18 Canberra T.17s)

RAF Wyton, Cambridgeshire
39 Squadron (- Canberra PR.9s)
51 Squadron (3 Comet C.2RCs, 4 Canberra B.6RCs)
543 Squadron (8 Victor SR.2s)

No. 38 Air Support Group
HQ RAF Benson, Oxfordshire

RAF Coningsby, Lincolnshire
6 Squadron (10 Phantom FGR.2s)
41 Squadron (10 Phantom FGR.2s)
54 Squadron (10 Phantom FGR.2s)

RAF Wittering, Peterborough
1 Squadron (15 Harrier GR.1s and GR.3s)
45 Squadron (9 Hunter FGA.9s)
58 Squadron (9 Hunter FGA.9s)

RAF Odiham, Hampshire
33 Squadron (13 Puma HC.1s)
72 Squadron (16 Wessex HC.2s)
230 Squadron (13 Puma HC.1s)
(Detachments to RAF Aldergrove, Northern Ireland)

46 Air Support Group
HQ Upavon, Wiltshire

RAF Brize Norton, Oxfordshire
10 Squadron (13 VC-10s)
53 Squadron (10 Belfasts)
99 Squadron (Britannia C.1s and Cs)
511 Squadron (Britannia C.1s and C.2s)
(20 Britannias operated by 99 and 511 Squadrons)

RAF Lyneham, Wiltshire
24 Squadron (Hercules C.1s)
30 Squadron (Hercules C.1s)
36 Squadron (Hercules C.1s)
47 Squadron (Hercules C.1s)

48 Squadron (Hercules C.1s)
(Total of 46 Hercules C.1s operated by the above squadrons)
216 Squadron (5 Comet C.4s)

RAF Thorney Island, Sussex
46 Squadron (15 Andover C.1s)

Other Strike Command Airfields
RAF Marham, Norfolk
In-flight refuelling wing
55 Squadron (Victor K.1s)
57 Squadron (Victor K.1s)
214 Squadron (Victor K.1s)
(Total of 28 Victors operated by the above squadrons)

RAF West Raynam
Target Facilities Unit
85 Squadron (13 Canberra B.2s and T.19s)
100 Squadron (13 Canberra B.2s and T.19s)

RAF St Mawgan, Cornwall
Target Facilities Unit
7 Squadron (18 Canberra B.2s and TT.18s)

Strike Command Operational Conversion Units (OCU) and Training Units
RAF Coltishall, Norfolk
226 OCU (65 Reserve Squadron) (26 Lightnings)
Battle of Britain Memorial Flight (Spitfires and 1 Hurricane)

RAF Coningsby, Lincolnshire
228 OCU (64 Reserve Squadron) (30 Phantom FGR.2s)

RAF Chivenor, Devon
229 OCU and Weapons Training Unit (63, 79 and 234 reserve squadrons) (50 Hunter
F.6s, FGA.9s and T.7s, Meteor T.7s and F.8s, and 2 Chipmunk T.1s)

RAF Scampton, Lincolnshire
230 OCU and Bomber Development Unit (- Vulcan B.2s)

RAF Cottesmore, Rutland
231 OCU (14 Canberra T.4s)

RAF Marham, Norfolk
232 OCU (5 Victor K.1s and B.2s)

RAF Wittering, Peterborough
233 OCU (20 Harrier GR.1s and T.2s)

RAF St Mawgan, Cornwall
236 OCU (5 Nimrod MR.1s)

RAF Honington (Suffolk)
237 OCU (12 Buccaneer S.2s, and 3 Hunter T.7s)

RAF Odiham, Hampshire
OCU (6 Puma HC.1s, and 5 Wessex HC.2s)

RAF Thorney Island, Sussex
242 OCU (8 Hercules C.1s, and 4 Andover C.1s)

RAF Brize Norton, Oxfordshire
241 OCU (VC-10s, Belfasts and Britannias transferred from based squadrons)

RAF Lossiemouth, Moray
[Relief landing ground: RAF Milltown]
OCU (6 Jaguar GR.1s and T.2s) (Additional aircraft in process of delivery – became 226 OCU)

RAF Scampton, Lincolnshire
Strike Command Bombing School (8 Hastings)

RAF Communications Squadrons

RAF Northolt, London
32 Squadron (1 Andover CC.2, 4 Basset CC.1s, 5 HS-125 CC.1s and CC.2s, and 6 Whirlwind HCC.12s)
207 Squadron (2 Pembroke C.1s, 8 Basset CC.1s and 5 Devon C.1s)
(Detachments: 1 Devon C.1 at RAF Turnhouse (Edinburgh) and 1 Devon C.1 at RAF Lindholme)

RAF Wyton, Cambridgeshire
26 Squadron (7 Basset CC.1s, and 5 Devon C.1s)

RAF Andover, Hampshire
21 Squadron (10 Devon C.1s, and 3 Pembroke C.1s)
(Also training on RAF communications aircraft was undertaken here)

RAF Benson, Oxfordshire
The Queen's Flight (3 Andover CC.2s, and 2 Wessex HCC.4s)

Station Flights

Many RAF stations had station flights. The aircraft were often Chipmunk T.10s, as at RAF Cranwell and RAF St Mawgan. Some, however, had other aircraft. RAF Wyton had Canberras and RAF Coningsby even had an Auster AOP.6. Also, many air stations had a gate guardian, often a Spitfire but sometimes a jet aircraft, at the entrance to the airfield.

RAF Support Command

HQ RAF Andover, Hampshire

Although most barrage balloons had disappeared from the skies over Britain at the end of the Second World War, a small number were retained for training parachutists. This example was giving a demonstration in Holyrood Park in Edinburgh in 1979.

Looking rather worse for wear are Hunter F.1 WT566 and Meteor T.7 WA697, used for the training of firemen at RAF Catterick in 1971.

Maintenance Units
RAF Kemble, Gloucestershire
5 MU (Andover, Argosy, Canberra, Harrier, Hunter, Meteor, Pembroke, Varsity.
2 Varsity T.1s, flown as 'hack' aircraft)

RAF St Athan, Vale of Glamorgan
19 and 32 MU (Buccaneer, Chipmunk, Gnat, Hunter, Nimrod, Shackleton, Victor,
Vulcan)

RAF Aldergrove, Northern Ireland
23 MU (Argosy, Canberra, Phantom, Varsity)

RAF Leconfield, Yorkshire
60 MU (Belfast, Britannia, Hasting, Lightning)

RAF Colerne, Wiltshire
MU (Hercules)

RAF Sydenham, Belfast
MU (Buccaneer, Sea Vixen)

RAF Bicester, Oxfordshire
71 MU (Repair of damaged and salvaged aircraft)

RAF Sealand, Flintshire
49 MU

RAF Cardington, Bedfordshire
271 MU (Filling and repair of gas cylinders for the military)
Also store of reserved aircraft for the RAF Museum

Schools of Technical Training
RAF Cosford
No. 1 School of Technical Training (4 Chipmunk T.10s, 2 Varsity T.1s)
Non-flying instructional aircraft: 1 Vulcan, 1 Victor, 2 Javelins, 1 Lightning,
3 Canberras, 1 Shackleton MR.2, 4 Shackleton MR.3s, 1 Sycamore
Also collection of RAF Museum aircraft

RAF Halton
No. 2 School of Technical Training (4 Chipmunk T.10s)
Non-flying instructional aircraft: 10 Sea Hawks, 20 Sea Vixens, 20 Provosts, 17 Jet
Provosts, 4 Canberras, 2 Hunters, 1 Gnat, 1 Twin Pioneers, 4 Sycamores

RAF St Athan, Vale of Glamorgan
No. 4 School of Technical Training
Non-flying instructional aircraft: 1 Argosy, 4 Buccaneers, - Canberras, 1 Chipmunk,
9 Hunters, 1 Lightning, 7 Pembrokes, 3 Vampires
Also collection of RAF Museum aircraft

RAF Locking, North Somerset
School of Technical Training

Other RAF Stations

RAF Henlow, Bedfordshire
Officer Training School

RAF Catterick
RAF Regiment Depot
RAF Fire Fighting and Rescue Squadron (Numerous derelict aircraft scattered around airfield for this purpose)

RAF Newton, Nottinghamshire
RAF Police Training School

RAF Hullavington, Wiltshire
Parachute packing unit

RAF Abingdon, Oxfordshire
No. 1 Parachute Training School
(RAF Andovers operated out of this airfield in support of this role)

RAF Weston-on-Green, Oxfordshire
Drop zone for parachute training

RAF Spitalgate, Lincolnshire
RAF Central Gliding School
(RAF Gliding Schools were located at some 30 locations throughout the British Isles on RAF airfields)

Stornoway, Western Isles
Reserve NATO Airfield

RAF Fairford
Concorde test flights

RAF Hendon
RAF Museum

Master Diversion Airfields
RAF Aldergrove, Northern Ireland

RAF Manston, Kent

RAF Machrihanish, Argyll and Bute

RAF Radar Stations with an Airfield
RAF Bishops Court, County Down, Northern Ireland

RAF Lindholme, Yorkshire
RAF North Luffenham, Rutland
RAF Watton, Norfolk

Weapon Ranges
RAF Pembrey Sands Air Weapons Range, Carmarthenshire

RAF Tain Air Weapons Range, Ross and Cromarty

Overseas RAF Airfields

RAF Germany
HQ Rheindahlen

RAF Bruggen
14 Squadron (13 Phantom FGR.2s)
17 Squadron (12 Phantom FGR.2s)
31 Squadron (13 Phantom FGR.2s)
No. 431 MU

RAF Gutersloh
19 Squadron (17 Lightning F.2s)
92 Squadron (14 Lightning F.2s)
18 Squadron (13 Wessex HC.2s)

RAF Laarbruck
2 Squadron (10 Phantom FGR.2s)
15 Squadron (15 Buccaneer S.2s)
16 Squadron (14 Buccaneer S.2s)

A Canberra B(I).8 of 3 Squadron, RAF Germany, at RAF Leuchars in 1971. Over the next few years the Canberra was replaced in the bomber role by Buccaneer S.2s and Phantoms.

RAF Wildenrath
3 Squadron (13 Harrier GR.1s and GR.3s)
4 Squadron (12 Harrier GR.1s and GR.3s)
20 Squadron (11 Harrier GR.1s and GR.3s)
60 Squadron (8 Pembroke C.1s, 1 Andover CC.2)
18 Squadron (4 Wessex HC.2s) (detachment)
Station Flight (Hunter T.7)

RAF Gatow (Berlin)
No based aircraft

RAF Near East
HQ RAF Eiskopi

RAF Akrotiri, Cyprus
9 Squadron (8 Vulcan B.2s)
35 Squadron (8 Vulcan B.2s)
56 Squadron (16 Lightning F.6s, 2 Canberras)
70 Squadron (6 Hercules C.1s, 2 Argosy C.1s)
84 Squadron (- Whirlwind HAR.10s)
103 MU

RAF Gibraltar, Gibraltar
229 OCU detachment (2–4 Hunters)

RAF Luqa, Malta
13 Squadron (12 Canberra PR.7s and R.9s)
203 Squadron (5 Nimrod MR.1s)

RAF Far East

RAF Masirah, Oman
(Staging post)
46 Squadron detachment (2 Andover C.1s)

RAF Gan, Indian Ocean
(Staging post)
No based aircraft

RAF Tengah, Singapore
103 Squadron (- Wessex HC.2s)

RAF Kai-Tak, Hong Kong
28 Squadron (- Wessex HC.2s)

Canada
RAF Goose Bay, Labrador
Staging post and training airfield

Fleet Air Arm (Including Royal Marines)

The Phantom Operation Conversion Unit was formed in September 1972 at RAF Leuchars to train pilots for 892 Squadron, deployed on HMS *Ark Royal*. One of the small number of aircraft used by this unit was this Phantom FG.1, XV570. It was unusual to train Royal Navy pilots in RAF aircraft which were painted in Royal Navy colours.

Three Buccaneer S.2s of 809 Squadron in 1973.

Built in 1961, this Gannet AEW.3, XL502, was one of forty-four examples built. It remained in service until 1978, when this type was withdrawn from service. It is shown here in 1975.

A Royal Navy Westland Sea King, XV656 of 819 Squadron, demonstrates its ability to carry military equipment in the form of a Land Rover at Prestwick Airport in June 1975.

Aircraft in Service

9 de Havilland Chipmunk T.10s
4 de Havilland Sea Vixen FAW.2s
4 de Havilland Sea Heron C.20s
10 de Havilland Sea Devon C.20s
14 Fairey Gannet AEW.3s
5 Fairey Gannets (COD.4s and T.5s)
8 Hunting Sea Prince T.1s
4 Hunting Sea Prince C.1s
7 English Electric Canberra T.22s
7 Hawker Hunter GA.11s
12 Hawker Hunter T.8s
15 Hawker Siddeley Buccaneer S.2s
15 McDonnell Douglas Phantom FG.1s

Helicopters in Service

20 Bell Sioux
12 Hiller HTG.2s
56 Westland Sea King HAS.1s
3 Westland Gazelles
6 Westland Scout AH.1s
75 Westland Wasp HAS.1s
25 Westland Whirlwinds (HAS.7s, HAR.1s and HAR.3s)
150 Westland Wessexes (HAS.1s, HAS.3s and HU.5s)

Ship-Based Units

HMS *Ark Royal* (aircraft carrier)
809 Squadron (14 Buccaneers)
892 Squadron (12 Phantoms)
849 Squadron (4 B Flight Gannet AEW.3s, 1 Gannet COD.4)
824 Squadron (6 Sea King HAS.1s)
Ship's Flight (2 Wessex HAS.1s)

HMS *Bulwark* and HMS *Hermes* (Commando carriers)
16 Wessex HU.5s each from 845 or 848 Squadron
4 Sea Kings from 814 Squadron

HMS *Fearless* and HMS *Intrepid* (assault ships)
6 Wessex HU.5s each from 845, 846 or 848 Squadron

HMS *Blake* (helicopter and command cruiser)
820 Squadron (4 Sea King HAS.1s)

HMS *Tiger* (helicopter and command cruiser)
826 Squadron (4 Sea King HAS.1s)

County Class Destroyers (8)
Each with one Wessex HAS.3

Leander Class Frigates (27)
Each with one Wasp HAS.1 of 829 Squadron

Tribal Class Frigates (7)
Each with one Wasp HAS.1 of 829 Squadron

Rothesay Class Frigates (9)
Some with one Wasp HAS.1 of 829 Squadron

HMS *Engadine* and HMS *Lofoten* (helicopter training ships)
Each capable of accommodating 6 Wessexes

Survey/Patrol Ships (4)
Each with one Wasp HAS.1 of 829 Squadron

Fleet Supply Ships (2)
Each with one Wessex HU.5 on detachment

Fleet Supply Tankers (3)
Each with one Wessex HU.5 on detachment

A number of other Royal Navy ships have helicopter landing pads but have no machine based aboard.

Fleet Air Arm Shore Bases

Royal Marines Condor, Angus
2–3 Sioux attached to 45 Commando

Royal Marines Coypool, Plymouth
3 Commando Air Brigade Squadron (6 Scout AH.1s, 16 Sioux)

RAF Cottesmore, Rutland
360 Squadron Canberras operated jointly by RAF and Royal Navy

RNAS Culdrose, Cornwall
[Relief landing ground: RNAS Perranporth]

705 Squadron (12 Hiller HT2s, 2 Gazelles, 15 Whirlwinds)
706 Squadron (6 Sea King HAS.1s, 5 Wasp HAS.1Hs)
750 Squadron (6 Sea Prince T.1s)
Station Flight (5 Whirlwinds, 1 Sea Devon C.20, 1 Chipmunk T.10)

Home base for the following squadrons when disembarked:
820 Squadron (HMS *Blake*) (Sea King HAS.1s)

824 Squadron (HMS *Ark Royal*) (Sea King HAS.1s)
826 Squadron (HMS *Tiger*) (Sea King HAS.1s)

School of Aircraft Handling (Non-flying aircraft including Buccaneers, Gannets, Sea Hawks and Sea Vixens)

RNAY Fleetlands, Hampshire
Repairs and maintenance on Army, RAF and RN helicopters

RNAY Almondbank, Perthshire
Repair and maintenance of helicopters delivered by road. No landing facilities here.

RAF Honington, Suffolk
Shore base for 809 Squadron (15 Buccaneer S.2s)

RAF Leuchars, Fife
Shore base for 892 Squadron (15 Phantom FG.1s)
Phantom Operation Conversion Unit (Combined RAF and RN training unit)

RAF Lossiemouth, Moray
849 Squadron (10 Gannet AEW.3s, 4 Gannet T.5s, COD.4)
Shore base for B Flight (4 Gannet AEW.3s, 1 Gannet COD.1)

RNAS Lee-on-Solent, Hampshire
781 Squadron (4 Sea Heron C.20s, 8 Sea Devon C.20s, 2 Wessexes)

Plymouth (Roborough) Airport, Plymouth
(8 Chipmunk T.10s)

RNAS Portland, Dorset
703 Squadron (6 Wasp HAS.1s)
737 Squadron (6 Sea King HAS.1s, 7 Wessex HAS.3s)
771 Squadron (10 Wessex HAS.1s)
829 Squadron (4 Wasps, HQ Flight)
Also shore base for nearly 50 ship-based flights equipped with Wasps

RNAS Prestwick, Ayrshire
819 Squadron (6 Sea King HAS.1s)
Shore base for 814 Squadron (4 Sea King HAS.1s)

RAF Sydenham, Belfast
30 Sea Vixens in storage
Station Flight: 1 Sea Devon C.20

RNAS Yeovilton, Somerset
[Relief landing ground: RNAS Merryfield]
HQ Fleet Air Arm

707 Squadron (12 Wessex HU.5s)

846 (HQ) Squadron (8 Wessex HU.5s and 1 Wasp HAS.1)
Shore base for 845 Squadron (20 Wessex HU.5s and 1 Wasp HAS.1)
846 Squadron (20 Wessex HU.5s and 1 Wasp HAS.1s)

Fleet Requirements and Aircraft Direction Unit (FRADU) (7 Canberra T.22s, 7 Hunter GA.11s, 12 Hunter T.8s, 4 Sea Vixen FAW.2s)

Station Flight: 2 Chipmunk T.10s, 1 Devon C.20, 1 Sea Prince, 1 Wessex

Fleet Air Arm Museum

RNAY Wroughton, Swindon
Repairs and maintenance of Army, RAF and Royal Navy helicopters

Army Air Corps

A rare example of a Chipmunk T.10 in a camouflaged colour scheme. This example, WP964, is at RAF Greenham Common in 1976.

The Westland (Agusta-Bell) Sioux was the Army Air Corps' main helicopter at the beginning of the 1970. By the end of the decade, however, it had been replaced by the Westland Gazelle and Lynx.

Aircraft in Service

2 Auster AOP.9s
24 de Havilland Chipmunk T.10s
30 de Havilland Beaver AL.1s

Helicopters in Service

10 Alouette IIs
4 Westland Gazelle AH.1s
120 Westland Scout AH.1s
175 Agusta-Bell Sioux AH.1s

Airfields

AAC Middle Wallop, Hampshire
Army Aviation Centre
Initial Fixed Wing Flight (24 Chipmunk T.10s)
Advanced Fixed Wing Flight (4 Beaver AL.1s, 2 Auster AOP.9s)
Initial Rotary Wing Flight (20 Sioux – civil helicopters operated by Bristows)
Advanced Rotary Wing Flight (25 Sioux AH.1s, 10 Scout AH.1s)
Intensive Flying Unit (4 Gazelles)
Maintenance School (Sioux, Austers, etc. for ground instruction)
70 Command (REME) Workshops (Overhaul and 1st and 2nd line repairs)
Army Air Corps Museum

In 1973, the Army Air Corps had a total of 160 aircraft and helicopters based in the British Isles. In addition to AAC Middle Wallop, there were units based at the following locations:

Airfields: AAC Netheravon, Wiltshire; AAC Old Sarum, Wiltshire; RAF Topcliffe, Yorkshire; RAE Farnborough, Hampshire.

Barracks and Army Bases: Barnard Castle, Durham; Catterick Camp, Yorkshire; Colchester, Essex; Hereford, Herefordshire; Larkhill, Wiltshire; Perham Down, Wiltshire; Warminster, Wiltshire.

Army Air Corps Overseas Bases

Units equipped with Beaver AL.1s, Scout AH.1s and Sioux AH.1s were based at the following locations:

Germany: Berlin, Bunde, Detmold (HQ), Iserlohn, Osnabruck, Minden, Munster, Soltau, Verden, Wildenrath.

Near East (Cyprus): Dhekelia, Nicosia.

Far East: Hong Kong, Kluang, Singapore (HQ); Kuching, Sarawak, Malacca, Malaysia; Seletar, Sembawang, Singapore.

Canada: Suffield Ranges, Alberta.

Military Research and Test Airfields

Although the Gloster Javelin was retired from RAF service in 1967, XH897, a FAW.9, pictured here, continued in service with A&AEE, Boscombe Down, until 1974. It is pictured here shortly before its retirement.

The RAF Institute of Aviation Hawker Hunter T.7 XL651, at RAF Greenham Common in 1976. This aircraft was normally based at Farnborough.

Aeroplane and Armament Experimental Establishment

Boscombe Down, Wiltshire

A&AEE divided into 8 divisions, of which two were concerned with flying and testing aircraft and equipment:

(A) Flying Division

1. A Squadron, responsible for high-performance aircraft and equipped with Buccaneer S.2s, Meteor, 1 Javelin, 1 Phantom, etc.
2. B Squadron, responsible for bombers and maritime aircraft and equipped with a large number of various versions of the Canberra, also Vulcan, etc.
3. D Squadron, responsible for all helicopters including Sea Kings, Wessexes and Whirlwinds.
4. E Squadron, responsible for transport aircraft and which also provided support flight for ferrying equipment and personnel. Its aircraft included an Argosy, a Comet 4, a Britannia and a Hercules.

(B) Several lodger units including the Joint Services Trials Unit, which were allocated aircraft from the Flying Division: 3 North American Harvards

(C) Empire Test Pilots' School: 1 Argosy, 2 Bassets, 3 Canberras, 1 Chipmunk T.10, 5 Hunters, 1 Lightning, 1 Twin Pioneer, 1 Scout AH1, 1 Wessex, 1 Whirlwind

Royal Radar Establishment, Pershore, Worcestershire
9 Canberras, 1 Hastings, 1 Meteor, 1 Puma, 2 Varsity, 2 Viscounts

Royal Aircraft Establishment Aberporth, Ceredigon
Missile test facility with airfield used by communications aircraft

Royal Aircraft Establishment Bedford, Bedfordshire
1 Auster AOP, 1 BAC-111, 1 Canberra, 1 Gnat, 1 HS-125, 1 Hunter, 1 Hunting H.126, 4 Sea Vixens, 1 Scout, 1 Shorts SC1, 1 VC-10, 2 Wessex

Royal Aircraft Establishment Farnborough, Hampshire
- Canberras, 1 Comet C.4, 3 Devons, - Hastings, 4 Hunter T.7s, - Meteor, - Scout, 1 Varsity, - Wessex

Meteorological Flight (lodger unit): 1 Hercules, 1 Varsity, 1 Canberra R.3

Royal Aircraft Establishment Llanbedr, Gwynedd
2 Canberras B.2 and PR.3, 1 Devon, 1 Hunter, - Meteor T.7 and T.20, - Meteor U.16 drones, 2 Sea Vixen FAW.2s

Royal Aircraft Establishment West Freugh, Dumfries and Galloway
2 C-47 Dakotas

Military Aircraft Manufacturers

Scottish Aviation Jetstream T.2 XX489 at Prestwick Airport in June 1975, awaiting delivery to the RAF.

A British Aerospace Hawk T.1, XX205, in RAF markings on display at the Farnborough Airshow in 1978. Although it was designed as a trainer it could also be used in the ground-attack role. Some of the weapons it was capable of carrying are displayed in front of the aircraft.

British Aircraft Corporation

Filton Airfield, South Gloucestershire
Overhauls of military aircraft
Rolls-Royce Research Flight (military aircraft on loan from military units)

Samlesbury Airfield, Lancashire
Canberra conversions and overhauls

Warton Airfield, Lancashire.
Research and production of the Tornado
Production of the Jaguar and Strike Masters
Overhaul of BAC aircraft in military service

Hawker Siddeley Aviation

Bitteswell Airfield, Leicestershire
Vulcan conversions

Brough Airfield, Yorkshire
Assembly of Buccaneers

Dunsfold Airfield, Surrey
Assembly of Harriers and test flying
Hunter overhauls and conversions

Holme-on-Spalding Airfield, Yorkshire
Conversions and test flying of Buccaneers and Phantoms

Woodford Airfield, Greater Manchester
Nimrod production, Victor conversions

Ferranti Flying Unit

Edinburgh Airport
Canberra, 1 Meteor

Flight Refuelling Ltd

Tarrant Rushton Airfield, Dorset
Conversions of aircraft for flight refuelling, overhauls, Sea Vixen conversions for RAE

Short Brothers

West Malling Airfield
Overhauls of RAF Varsity and DH Chipmunk aircraft
Ferry flight operated 3 Varsities in RAF markings

Martin Baker Aircraft Ltd

Chalgrove Airfield, Oxfordshire
2 Meteor T.7s operated for testing ejection seats

Scottish Aviation Limited

Prestwick Airport, Ayrshire
Production and test flights of Bulldogs and Jetstreams

Westland Helicopters

Yeovil, Somerset
Production and test flights of Sea Kings and Lynx

Weston-super-Mare Airfield, North Somerset
Production of Gazelle helicopters

US Air Force Squadrons Based in Britain

A Phantom F-4D of the USAF 48th TFW at RAF Lakenheath in 1973. The D variant of the aircraft was produced in greater numbers than almost all others.

At the beginning of the 1970s, the USAF still had a considerable number of North American F-100 Super Sabre fighter bombers based in Britain at RAF Lakenheath and RAF Upper Heyford. Their days, however, were numbered and the last example departed in early 1972, being replaced by Phantoms and F-111s. The F-100F Super Sabre pictured here in 1970 is S6-3884 of 48 TFW from RAF Lakenheath.

US Aircraft based in Britain

 - Bell Iroquois
4 Boeing EC-135
6 Convair T-29
78 General Dynamics F-111E
16 Lockheed Hercules (on detachment)
9 Lockheed C-130T and N Hercules
1 North American T-39 Sabeliner
4 Lockheed T-33
4 Sikorsky HH-53C
210 McDonnell Douglas Phantoms F-4C, F-4D and F-4E

US Naval Aircraft

3 Convair C-131
1 Grumman C-1 Trader

RAF Alconbury, Cambridgeshire
10th Tactical Reconnaissance Wing (1st Tactical Reconnaissance Squadron, 30th Tactical Reconnaissance Squadron, 32nd Tactical Reconnaissance Squadron) (65 RF-4C Phantoms)
Detachment of 4 T-33s

RAF Bentwaters, Suffolk
81st Tactical Fighter Wing (91st Tactical Fighter Squadron, 92nd Tactical Fighter Squadron) (50 F-4C Phantoms)

RAF Greenham Common, West Berkshire
Reserve airfield used for military exercises

RAF Lakenheath, Suffolk
48th Tactical Fighter Wing (492nd Tactical Fighter Squadron, 493rd Tactical Fighter Squadron, 494th Tactical Fighter Squadron) (70 F-4D Phantoms)

RAF Mildenhall, Suffolk
513th Tactical Airlift Wing (16 C-130 Hercules – 2 Squadrons on rotation from USA)
10th ACCS (4 EC-135)
Detachments of KC-135 from USA
Headquarters, 3rd Air Force (6 T-29G, 1 T-39)
US Navy (NAF Mildenhall) (1 C-1 Trader, 3 C-131)

RAF Sculthorpe, Norfolk
Reserve airfield used for military exercises

RAF Upper Heyford, Oxfordshire
20th Tactical Fighter Wing (55th Tactical Fighter Squadron, 77th Tactical Fighter Squadron, 79th Tactical Fighter Squadron) (78 F-111E)

RAF Wethersfield, Essex
Reserve airfield used by F-4 Phantoms

RAF Woodbridge, Suffolk
81st Tactical Fighter Wing (30 F-4D Phantoms)
78th Tactical Fighter Wing
67 Aerospace Rescue and Recovery Squadron (9 HC-130 H/P Hercules, 4 HH-53)

US Army Depot Burntonwood
2 Iroquois (on detachment from Germany)

Other Foreign Military Aircraft Based in Britain

RAF Chivenor, Devon
3–4 Hunters of the Singapore Air Defence based here for training purposes

Prestwick Airport, Ayrshire
Canadian Armed Forces F-104 Starfighters and T-33s based in Western Germany serviced by Scottish Aviation Limited.

Bibliography

Balch, Adrian M., *Testing Colours – British Test, Trials and Research Aircraft of A&AEE, RAE & ETPS since 1960*, Airlife Publishing Ltd, Shrewsbury, 1993.

Beaver, Paul, *Today's Army Air Corps*, Patrick Stephens, 1987.

Brookes, Andrew, *Vulcan Units of the Cold War*, Osprey Combat Aircraft No. 72, Osprey Publishing, Oxford, 4th impression, 2013.

British Naval and Army Aviation 1969, West London Aviation Group, Middlesex, 1969.

Delve, Ken, *The Source Book of the RAF*, Airlife Publishing Ltd, Shrewsbury, 1994.

Darling, Kev, *RAF Strike Command 1968–2007: Aircraft, Men and Action*, Pen & Sword Books, Barnsley, South Yorkshire, 2012.

Mills, Wendy, *Target Rolling – A History of Llanbedr Airfield*, Midland Publishing, Hinckley, 2002.

Pocock, Chris, and Colin Smith, *The USAF Today*, West London Aviation Group, Middlesex, 1975.

Taylor, J. W. R., *Warplanes of the World*, Ian Allan, London, 1966.

The Royal Air Force 1971, West London Aviation Group, Middlesex, 1971.

Thetford, Owen, *Aircraft of the Royal Air Force Since 1918*, Putnam Aeronautical Books, London, 1995 edition.

Thetford, Owen, *British Naval Aircraft Since 1912*, Putnam & Company, London, 1971.

U.S. Military Aviation in Europe, 1970, West London Aviation Group, Middlesex, 1970.

Watkins, David, *The History of RAF Aerobatic Teams From 1920*, Pen & Sword Books Ltd, Barnsley, South Yorkshire, 2010.

Websites

Flightarchives